Contents

Sound Sheet 1

Read these sounds with your teacher.
Read and memorize the first group of vowel sounds and key words.
After you have memorized one group of sounds, move on to the next group.
Always start with the first group for review. Check each group as you learn it.

____ 1. ***a*** says /ă/ as in *apple*.
a says /ā/ as in *baby* at the end of an open syllable *(ba/by)*.
a says /ô/ as in *all* and after some *qu*'s and *w*'s as in *quality* and *water*.

____ 2. ***e*** says /ĕ/ as in *elephant*.
e says /ē/ as in *recess* at the end of an open syllable *(re/cess)*.

____ 3. ***i*** says /ĭ/ as in *it*.
i says /ī/ as in *spider* at the end of an open syllable *(spi/der)*.

____ 4. ***o*** says /ŏ/ as in *ox*.
o says /ō/ as in *pony* at the end of an open syllable *(po/ny)*.
o says /ŭ/ as in *other*.

____ 5. ***u*** says /ŭ/ as in *up*.
u says /ū/ as in *music* at the end of an open syllable *(mu/sic)*.
u says /o͝o/ as in *put*.

____ 6. ***y*** says /ĭ/ as in *gym*.
y says /ī/ as in *cyclone* at the end of an open syllable *(cy/clone)*.
y says /ē/ as in *candy* at the end of a word.
y says /ī/ as in *sky* at the end of a word.

____ 7. ***y*** is a consonant when it begins a word. **y** says /y/ as in *yes* when it begins a word.

Vowel-Consonant-e

____ 8. ***a***-consonant-***e*** says /ā/ as in *safe*.
e-consonant-***e*** says /ē/ as in *these*.
i-consonant-***e*** says /ī/ as in *pine*.

____ 9. ***o***-consonant-***e*** says /ō/ as in *home*.
u-consonant-***e*** says /ū/ as in *mule*.
y-consonant-***e*** says /ī/ as in *type*.

Sound Sheet 2

Read these sounds with your teacher.
Read and memorize each sound and its key word(s).
Check each group as you learn it.

____ 1. ***sh*** says /sh/ as in *ship.*

____ 2. ***ch*** says /ch/ as in *chin.*
ch says /k/ as in *chorus.*
ch says /sh/ as in *Chicago.*

____ 3. ***th*** says /t̶h̶/ as in *this.*
th says /th/ as in *thin.*

____ 4. ***wh*** says /hw/ as in *white.*

____ 5. ***qu*** says /kw/ as in *queen.*

____ 6. ***ph*** says /f/ as in *phone.*

____ 7. ***c*** says /k/ as in cat.
c says /s/ when it comes before e, *i*, or *y*.

____ 8. ***g*** says /g/ as in *go.*
g usually says /j/ when it comes before e, *i*, or *y*. (*Get, give, girl,* and *gift* are exceptions.)

____ 9. ***s*** says /s/ as in *sat.*
s between two vowels says /z/ as in *nose.*
s at the end of some short words says /z/ as in *is, as,* and *has.*
s says /z/ when it makes a word possessive, as in *Tom's cap* and *the boy's cat.*

____ 10. ***x*** says /ks/ as in *box.*
x says /gz/ as in *exist.*

____ 11. ***y*** says /y/ as in *yes* when it begins a word.

____ 12. ***ed*** says /ĕd/ as in *rented.*
ed says /d/ as in *sailed.*
ed says /t/ as in *jumped.*

____ 13. ***ck*** says /k/ as in *black* at the end of a word or syllable directly after a single short vowel.

____ 14. ***tch*** says /ch/ as in *catch* at the end of a word or syllable directly after a single short vowel.

____ 15. ***dge*** says /j/ as in *fudge* at the end of a word or syllable directly after a single short vowel.

____ 16. ***tion*** says /shŭn/ as in *station.*
tion says /chŭn/ as in *question.*

____ 17. ***sion*** says /shŭn/ as in *discussion.*
sion says /zhŭn/ as in *television.*
sion says /chŭn/ as in *comprehension.*

____ 18. ***old*** says /ōld/ as in *bold.*

____ 19. ***ng*** says /ng/ as in *sing.*

Sound Sheet 3

Read these sounds with your teacher.
Read and memorize each sound and its key word(s).
Check each group as you learn it.

The first sound given is the more common sound.

____ 1. ***ay*** says /ā/ as in *play* at the end of a word.

____ 2. ***ai*** says /ā/ as in *aid* and *sail* at the beginning or in the middle of a word.

____ 3. ***ow*** says /ō/ as in *snow*.
ow says /ou/ as in *plow*.

____ 4. ***ou*** says /ou/ as in *out*.
ou says /o͞o/ as in *soup*.

____ 5. ***oo*** says /o͞o/ as in *food*.
oo says /o͝o/ as in *book*.

____ 6. ***oy*** says /oi/ as in *toy* at the end of a word.
oi says /oi/ as in *oil* and *boil* at the beginning or in the middle of a word.

____ 7. ***oa*** says /ō/ as in *boat*.

____ 8. ***oe*** says /ō/ as in *toe*.

____ 9. ***ee*** says /ē/ as in *feed*.

____ 10. ***igh*** says /ī/ as in *light*.

____ 11. ***aw*** says /ô/ as in *saw*.

____ 12. ***au*** says /ô/ as in *August*.

____ 13. ***ie*** says /ē/ as in *chief*.
ie says /ī/ as in *pie*.

____ 14. ***ea*** says /ē/ as in eat.
ea says /ĕ/ as in *bread*.
ea says /ā/ as in *steak*.

____ 15. ***eigh*** says /ā/ as in *eight*.

____ 16. ***ew*** says /ū/ as in *few*.
ew says /o͞o/ as in *grew*.

____ 17. ***ey*** says /ē/ as in *valley*.
ey says /ā/ as in *they*.

____ 18. ***ue*** says /ū/ as in *rescue*.
ue says /o͞o/ as in *true*.

____ 19. ***ei*** says /ē/ as in *ceiling*.
ei says /ā/ as in *vein*.

____ 20. ***eu*** says /ū/ as in *feud*.

____ 21. ***er*** says /er/ as in *her*.

____ 22. ***ir*** says /er/ as in *bird*.

____ 23. ***ur*** says /er/ as in *burn*.

____ 24. ***ear*** says /er/ as in *learn*.

____ 25. ***or*** says /or/ as in *hornet*.
or says /er/ as in *doctor*.
or after the letter *w* usually says /er/ as in *word*.

____ 26. ***ar*** says /är/ as in *car*.
ar says /er/ as in *beggar*.

Sounds of *c* and *g*

c before a, *o, u, l,* and *r* has the hard sound /k/. c before e, *i,* and y has the soft sound /s/.

g before a, *o, u, l,* and *r* has the hard sound /g/. *g* before e, *i,* and y usually has the soft sound /j/.

Read these words. Mark the sound of *c* or *g* as hard or soft after each word. Use the following symbols.

hard *c* = /k/ soft *c* = /s/ hard *g* = /g/ soft *g* = /j/

cinder	/s/	ceremony	______	graduation	______
gypsy	/j/	cylinder	______	geography	___ ___
gerbil	______	glimpse	______	calculate	___ ___
genius	______	gradual	______	complete	______
gaunt	______	clothes	______	container	______
climax	______	cardinal	______	gymnasium	______
cement	______	gosling	___ ___	cemetery	______
gurgle	___ ___	carnival	______	continent	______
gyrate	______	gondola	______	contingent	___ ___
census	______	century	______	condolence	___ ___
ginger	___ ___	cyclone	___ ___	glandular	______
gentle	______	generous	______	crocodile	___ ___
grouch	______	bicycle	___ ___	circumstance	___ ___ ___
celery	______	gullible	______	contagious	___ ___
catsup	______	gesture	______	contentment	______
giddy	______	cavalry	______	gigantic	___ ___ ___
general	______	category	___ ___	cellophane	______

Other Sounds for the Vowels *a* and *o*

Read these words. Check the words you cannot spell and study them. Then have your teacher test you on the words you checked.

1. *a* usually says /ô/ when followed by *l*.

ball	hall	small	talk	walnut	wallop
call	wall	halt	chalk	waltz	walrus
fall	tall	walk	stalk	wallet	

2. *a* usually says /ä/ after *w*.

wad	wand	waddle	watch	wasp	
wan	wander	waffle	watt		

a usually says /ô/ when followed by *r*; *r*-controlled words do not have the same sound as the group of words above.

war	ward	warm	wart	award	swarm
warble	warden	warp	wardrobe	reward	

3. *a* usually says /ä/ after *qu*.

qualify	qualm	quadruple	squad	squash	squander
quality	quadrangle	quadruplet	squat	squall	

a after *qu* says /ô/ if it is *r*-controlled.

quart	quarter	quarrel

4. *a* says /ŭ/ at the beginning of these words.

ahead	above	alike	around	asleep	aware
aboard	across	alive	award	afloat	amend
abound	afar	along	away	adrift	amaze
about	again	among	awhile	ashore	afraid

5. The underlined *a*'s in the following words say /ŭ/.

banana	idea	parade	umbrella	soda	coma
China	India	panda	vanilla	sofa	comma

6. *o* says /ŭ/ in these words.

other	come	love	ton	lion	lemon
mother	some	dove	son	Monday	diamond
brother	done	glove	won	month	somebody
another	none	shove	wonder	nothing	parrot
smother	oven	front	onion	tongue	wagon
	dozen				

7. *o* is not heard in the second syllable of these words.

lesson	mutton	cotton	carton	ribbon	glutton
button	bottom	atom			

Syllables

Read and learn.

A syllable is part of a word with a vowel in it. There are six kinds of syllables.

A syllable may be only one letter if the letter is a vowel *(I, a, o/pen)*. A syllable may be one small word *(in, rob, cry)*. A syllable may be part of a longer word *(in/vent, nap/kin)*.

A word usually has as many syllables as it has vowel sounds *(un/der/stand)*. Do not count *u* as a vowel when it appears after *q (ques/tion, quick)*.

Learn the six kinds of syllables listed below. Read and memorize each type of syllable and its description. Check each type of syllable after you have learned it.

The Six Kinds of Syllables

____ I. Closed syllable
- A. A closed syllable ends with a consonant.
- B. The vowel before the final consonant has a short sound *(thăt, shŏt, strŭt)*.

____ II. Open syllable
- A. An open syllable ends with a vowel.
- B. The vowel has a long sound. (The long sound of a vowel is usually the name of the vowel.)
- C. An open syllable can be just one letter if that letter is a vowel *(Ī, ā, ō/pen)*.

____ III. Vowel-consonant-e syllable
- A. The final e is silent in a vowel-consonant-e syllable.
- B. The silent e at the end of the word makes the vowel before it have a long sound *(mūle̸, sāme̸, strīpe̸)*.

____ IV. Diphthong syllable
- A. It usually has two vowels together that have one sound. (See Sound Sheet 3 on page 3.)
- B. The diphthong syllable has a special sound. You have already learned the sounds of the diphthongs on Sound Sheet 3 *(sail, stay, snow/ing, light, eight, greet/ing)*.
- C. Be sure to notice whether a vowel combination is reversed (for example, *io* instead of *oi*, as in *vi/o/lin)*. If the two vowels are reversed, divide between them.

____ V. *r*-combination syllable

A. The *r*-combination syllable always has at least one vowel followed by *r*. The *r* always comes directly *after* the vowel *(ar, er, ir, or, ur,* and *ear)*. The *r* gives the vowel a unique sound.

B. You have already learned the sounds these vowel-*r* combinations make *(start, bird, burn/ing, learn, her, port, doctor, beggar, work)*.

____ VI. Consonant-*le* syllable

A. This syllable always comes at the end of a word *(cra/dle, bub/ble, ti/tle)*.

B. The consonant-*le* syllable has no vowel sound. The silent e at the end of the syllable is the only vowel. Only the consonant and the *l* are pronounced.

Name the Syllables

1. **Underline all the sounded vowels and diphthongs. Cross out silent *e*'s.**
2. **Label all the syllables:**

o = open	d = diphthong	vc*e* = vowel-consonant-*e*
c = closed	r = *r*-combination	c-*le* = consonant-*le*

3. **Read the syllables orally.**

min	c	neer	______	crot	______	sor	______
gist	______	boit	______	phar	______	site	______
rod	______	pa	______	stra	______	slaw	______
sproy	______	chip	______	chade	______	zoot	______
tle	______	ho	______	gluve	______	frip	______
yox	______	ribe	______	grar	______	cres	______
gle	______	borst	______	zle	______	mane	______
quop	______	ri	______	hum	______	pone	______
ti	______	ple	______	arp	______	ron	______
leez	______	hus	______	taub	______	tro	______

Syllabication
(Dividing Words into Syllables)

Read with your teacher. Then read again and learn.

Here is a simple formula that you can follow for dividing words into syllables.

1. Underline all the sounded vowels and diphthongs. A single e at the end of a word is usually silent; cross out silent e's.
2. Count the sounded vowels. This tells you how many syllables are in the word.
3. See if the word contains a familiar suffix such as *-er, -ing, -ful,* or *-tion.* If so, separate this syllable from the rest of the word.
4. Label all vowels and consonants, starting with the first vowel.

Examples:	a n c e s t o r	j u v e n i l ~~e~~	t r i p p i n g
	v c c v c c v c	v c v c v c	v c c v c c

5. See what *pattern* the vowels and consonants make: VCCV, VCV, or VCCCV.
   - A. Whenever *two consonants* come together in a word, divide between them: VC/CV. Do not divide blends.

Examples:	c o n / t e n t	a d / m i r ~~e~~	a t / m o s / p h e r ~~e~~
	v c / c v c c	v c / c v c	v c / c v c / c c v c

   - B. When only one consonant comes between two vowels, divide *after the first vowel:* V/CV. This makes an open syllable, and the vowel usually has a long sound.

Examples:	s i / l e n t	(not sil/ent)	v a / c a / t io n	(not vac/a/tion)
	v / c v c c		v / c v / c v c	

     Pronounce the word with an open syllable. If this does not make a word that sounds familiar, divide *after the consonant:* VC/V.

Examples:	l i m / i t	(not li/mit)	c a b / i n	(not ca/bin)
	v c / v c		v c / v c	

   - C. When three consonants come together, divide *after the first consonant:* VC/CCV. If this does not make a word that sounds familiar, divide after the second consonant: VCC/CV.

Examples:	c o m / p l e t ~~e~~	(not comp/lete)	p u m p / k i n	(not pum/pkin)
	v c / c c v c		v c c / c v c	

6. If a vowel combination is reversed, divide between the vowels. Each vowel will then have a sound.

Examples:	v i / o / l e t	v i / o / l i n	v i / o / l e n t	d i / a l
	p e / o / n y	n e / o n	t r u / a n t	l i / a r

7. A few words have the pattern VCCCCV.

Examples:	s u b / s c r i b ~~e~~	d i p h / t h o n g	a r t h / r i / t i s
	v c / c c c v c	v c c / c c v c c	v c c c / c v / c v c

Exercise

Directions:

1. Underline all the sounded vowels and diphthongs. Cross out silent *e*'s.
2. Count the sounded vowels. This tells you the number of syllables in the word.
3. Label all vowels and consonants, starting with the first vowel in each word.
4. Look for a pattern: VCV, VCCV, VCCCV. Look for two patterns in longer words.
5. Follow the directions you have learned for dividing: V/CV or VC/V, VC/CV, VC/CCV or VCC/CV. Do not divide blends.
6. Label the syllables:

   o = open syllable
   c = closed syllable
   d = diphthong syllable
   v*ce* = vowel-consonant-*e*
   r = *r*-combination syllable
   c-*le* = consonant-*le* syllable

Remember: English is unpredictable. The main objective of syllabication is to decode the words so that you can pronounce them for reading and spelling.

mon|ster	com|plain	donate	meter
angry	harvest	surplus	compile
tonic	cradle[1]	counsel	trifle
electric	ancestor	publish	igloo
athlete	fragment	consonant	burglar
percolate	projectile	vocation	marvelous
opponent	exonerate	demolish	intrude
confirm	museum	equal[2]	extract
molasses	jonquil[2]	mattress	tomato

[1] This word does not divide between consonants (vc/cv) because the last syllable is a consonant-*le* syllable. In consonant-*le* syllables, count back three letters from the end of the word, draw a line, and then determine what kind of syllable begins the word.

[2] *qu* is considered one consonant because *q* is always followed by *u*. Then *u* is not considered a vowel.

Accenting Syllables

Read and learn.

When you pronounce a word made of two or more syllables, you usually say one syllable with more force than the others. This is called accenting a particular syllable. Hearing the accent on the correct syllable often gives you a clue about the identity of the word. If you do not hear a word that sounds familiar, try accenting a different syllable until your ears hear a familiar word. If you are unsure where the accent belongs, even after various experiments, you should look up the word in a dictionary.

These four accent patterns will help you determine which syllable is accented. Read them carefully and learn them.

1. Accent the root of a word. We usually do not accent the prefix or suffix.
   con/duct´/or pro/ject´/or sub/mit´ act´/ing
2. If there are two syllables in a root, accent the first syllable.
   sea´/son/ing
3. In words of three or more syllables that end in a silent-e syllable, there is usually one syllable between the accented syllable and the silent-e syllable.
   ex/on´/er/ate ap/pro´/pri/ate ac/cu´/mu/late con/tam´/i/nate
4. Some words can function both as verbs and as nouns or adjectives. In verbs the accent is usually on the root. In nouns and adjectives the accent is usually on the first syllable.

con/test´	re/bel´	re/cord´	sub/ject´
con´/test	reb´/el	rec´/ord	sub´/ject

Use a separate sheet of paper to write from memory the four accent patterns that help you determine which syllable in a word is accented.

Exercise

Place an accent mark on the correct syllable in these words.

ac/ces´/so/ry	dis/tract/ed	in/trude	va/ca/tion	neg/li/gent[1]
mir/a/cle	to/tal	plan/ta/tion	per/mis/sion	cos/met/ic
main/tain	mi/nus	a/ban/don/ment	an/nu/al	sub/sis/tence
mo/las/ses	mu/se/um	e/qual	ad/ven/ture	whole/sale

[1] *i* is an unstable letter. It does not always say /ī/ in an open syllable. It can also say /ĭ/ or /ē/.

Suffixes

A suffix is an ending added to a word. It changes the meaning of the word. Some suffixes begin with vowels, and some suffixes begin with consonants. A word without a suffix is called a base word.

Read and learn these suffixes.

Suffixes That Begin with Vowels

Suffix	Example	Suffix	Example
-ed[1]	rented, sailed, jumped	-ance	resistance, importance
-ing	sailing, taking	-ence	audience
-y	happy, dirty, candy	-est	reddest, highest
-er	redder, teacher	-ist	cyclist, novelist
-en	wooden, broken	-ary	secretary, ordinary
-al	verbal, musical	-ery	bakery, slavery
-ous	famous, nervous	-ory	dormitory, compulsory
-able	movable, breakable	-ish	boyish
-ible	divisible, edible	-ive	active
-ant	important	-ize	criticize, specialize
-ent	frequent, intelligent		

Suffixes That Begin with Consonants

Suffix	Example	Suffix	Example
-dom	kingdom, freedom	-ly	friendly, suddenly
-hood	boyhood, falsehood	-ment	amazement, enjoyment
-ful[2]	painful, cupful	-ship	friendship
-less	careless, homeless	-ty	loyalty
-ness	goodness, fitness	-ward	southward

[1] Remember that *-ed* as a suffix has three sounds: /ĕd/ as in *rented,* /d/ as in *sailed,* and /t/ as in *jumped.*
[2] When *-ful* is a suffix, it has only one *l.*

The Suffixes *-ful* and *-ly*

Read and learn.

-ful

1. The suffix *-ful* is spelled with just one *l*.
2. Add *ful* to base words without changing them. *-ful* means "full of." It forms adjectives and, sometimes, nouns.

   pain + ful = painful　　　　hand + ful = handful

-ly

1. Add *ly* to base words without changing them.
2. If the base word ends in *l*, there will be two *l*'s.

   total + ly = totally　　　　final + ly = finally

3. When adding *ly* to consonant-*le* words, drop the *le* and add *ly*.

   simple + ly = simply　　　　sensible + ly = ________

   double + ly = ________　　　　probable + ly = ________

   feeble + ly = ________　　　　possible + ly = ________

Add *ful* or *ly* to these words to make a new word.

general + ly = ________　　　　forcible + ly = ________

help + ful = ________　　　　swift + ly = ________

suitable + ly = ________　　　　thank + ful = ________

play + ful = ________　　　　usual + ly = ________

Read, copy, and learn.

Both *ful* and *ly* can be added to base words without changing them.

safe ________ safely ________

hope ________ hopeful ________ hopefully ________

use ________ useful ________ usefully ________

care ________ careful ________ carefully ________

peace ________ peaceful ________ peacefully ________

sorrow ________ sorrowful ________ sorrowfully ________

Sight Words

**Draw a line through the words you know how to spell.
Learn to spell all the words you do not know.
Look up the meaning of any word you cannot define.**

add
odd
answer
carry
marry
hurry
merry
ferry
berry
buy
busy
bury
dye
die
color
pretty
beauty
animal
minute
people
police
hero
during
laugh
walk
talk

chalk
lose
loose
very
every
else
easy
woman
women
above
canoe
ocean
change
strange
piano
promise
board
mitt
all right
almost
always
already

route
flood
blood
heart
tongue
move
prove
oh
owe
soul
usual
purpose
suppose
half (halves)
calf (calves)
wolf (wolves)
sure
sugar
orange
skiing
machine
spirit
clothes
material
broad
length
strength

special
especially
almighty
altogether
boulder
shoulder
group
troupe
tough
rough
enough
dough
cough
court
course
coarse
though
through
thorough
although
young
country
couple
touched
double
trouble

senior
straight
calm
palm
ache
iron
onion
salad
aisle
isle
island
juice
fruit
suit
cruise
bruise
biscuit
terrible
anxious
necessary
cousin
aunt
America
century
million
billion
bullion
bouillon

February
Wednesday
Fahrenheit
Celsius
imagine
engine
medicine
disease
vacuum
squirrel
mosquito
restaurant
library
guarantee
cordial
cereal
recipe
yacht
scissors
soldier
sergeant
lieutenant
colonel
bureau
spaghetti
chocolate
nuisance
capitol

Use a separate sheet of paper to write the sentences dictated by your teacher. The dictation will check your ability to spell all the sight words.[1]

[1] Dictate sentences from the lists on pages 49–50, 77–78, and 103–104 in *How to Teach Spelling*.

/k/—Spelled *k* and *ck*

The following generalizations will help you learn which letter(s) to use at the end of a word or syllable for the /k/ sound.

1. /k/ can be spelled *k* or *ck*.
2. Use *ck* at the end of a word or syllable directly after a single short vowel.
3. Use *k* after a consonant, after a long-vowel sound, and after two vowels.

Use a separate sheet of paper. Make two columns. Write *k* at the top of one column; write *ck* at the top of the other one. Write the words in the correct column.

shock	squeak	smoked	stroke	quack	stark
stuck	plucked	locket	blankly	thankful	darkly

Use a separate sheet of paper to write the sentences dictated by your teacher. This dictation will check your ability to spell words that end in *k* and *ck*.[1]

/ĭk/—Spelled *ic*

You already know that the /k/ sound directly after a single short vowel is spelled *ck*. Words with two or more syllables usually use *c* for the final /k/ sound.

Read these words, copy them on a separate sheet of paper, and learn them.

metric	public	atomic	antibiotic	ceramic
Arctic	electric	domestic	democratic	sympathetic
scenic	athletic	gigantic	mechanic	allergic
cubic	magnetic	olympic	scientific	automatic
tragic	elastic	Atlantic	systematic	specific
fabric	historic	Pacific	clinic	romantic
magic	heroic	frantic	arithmetic	gymnastic
music	attic	plastic	patriotic	terrific

Read and learn.

When adding a suffix that begins with e, *i*, or *y*, insert a *k* before the suffix to prevent the final c from being pronounced /s/.

picnic—picnicked—picnicking   panic—panicked—panicking
mimic—mimicked—mimicking   traffic—trafficked—trafficking

[1] Dictate sentences from the list on pages 40 and 41 in *How to Teach Spelling*.

/ch/—Spelled *ch* and *tch*

The following generalizations will help you learn which letters to use at the end of a word or syllable for the /ch/ sound.

1. /ch/ can be spelled *ch* or *tch*.
2. Use *tch* at the end of a word or syllable directly after a single short vowel.
3. Use *ch* at the beginning of a word, after a consonant, and after two vowels.
4. Exceptions to the generalizations are: *much, such, rich, which, sandwich, attach, detach,* and *ostrich*. Memorize them.

Use a separate sheet of paper. Make two columns. Write *ch* at the top of one column; write *tch* at the top of the other one. Write the words in the correct column.

trench	clutch	screeched	slouching	stretcher	stitching
scorched	ostrich	switched	pouches	catcher	sandwich

Use a separate sheet of paper to write the sentences dictated by your teacher. This dictation will check your ability to spell words that end in *ch* and *tch*.[1]

/j/—Spelled *ge* and *dge*

The following generalizations will help you learn which letters to use at the end of a word or syllable for the /j/ sound.

1. /j/ can be spelled *ge* or *dge*.
2. Use *dge* at the end of a word or syllable directly after a single short vowel.
3. Use *ge* after a consonant, after a long-vowel sound, and after two vowels.
4. Five words that have more than one syllable also follow these generalizations. They are: *partridge, cartridge, porridge, knowledge, acknowledge*. Learn them.

Use a separate sheet of paper. Make two columns. Write *ge* at the top of one column; write *dge* at the top of the other one. Write the words in the correct column.

sponges	trudge	arrange	lodges	cartridge	ridges
gorge	knowledge	largely	judges	merge	Scrooge
pledges	verge	nudge	smudge	ledges	hinges

Use a separate sheet of paper to write the sentences dictated by your teacher. This dictation will check your ability to spell words that end in *ge* and *dge*.[2]

[1] Dictate sentences from the list on pages 43 and 44 in *How to Teach Spelling*.

[2] Dictate sentences from the list on pages 45 and 46 in *How to Teach Spelling*.

/ĭj/—Spelled *age*

At the end of a word /ĭj/ is spelled age.

Read these words, copy them on a separate sheet of paper, and learn them.

baggage	cabbage	cottage	luggage	rummage
scrimmage	tonnage	cribbage	damage	manage
mileage	acreage	footage	yardage	average
advantage	bandage	coinage	courage	discourage
encourage	dosage	garbage	beverage	foliage
hostage	heritage	image	language	message
mortgage	orphanage	package	passage	pilgrimage
postage	salvage	sausage	savage	shortage
spoilage	storage	village	voltage	voyage
breakage	wreckage	ravage		

Copy and learn these two exceptions:

college ______________________ privilege ______________________

Use a separate sheet of paper to write the phrases and sentences dictated by your teacher. This dictation will check your ability to spell words that end in *age*.[1]

[1] Dictate phrases and sentences from the lists on pages 47 and 48 in *How to Teach Spelling*.

/ou/—Spelled *ou* and *ow*

Read and learn.

1. Use *ou* at the beginning or in the middle of a word unless the /ou/ sound is followed by a single *n*, *l*, *er*, or *el*; then use *ow*.

Examples:	flour	down	fowl	flower	towel
	shout	clown	growl	power	vowel
	ground	brown	scowl	tower	trowel

2. Use *ow* at the end of a word for the /ou/ sound.

Examples:	cow	now	plow	brow	allow

3. Learn the exceptions to these generalizations:

powder	chowder	crowd	coward	foul

Fill in the blanks with either *ou* or *ow*. Then read the words. Place a check in front of the words that are exceptions to the generalizations.

t_____el	m_____se	s_____r	pl_____	sc_____t
tr_____el	ar_____nd	p_____er	spr_____t	p_____der
c_____ard	fr_____n	sh_____er	cr_____d	gr_____l
f_____l	sl_____ch	f_____nd	fl_____er	tr_____sers
fl_____r	ch_____der	bl_____se	b_____nce	cr_____ch

Use a separate sheet of paper to write the phrases and sentences dictated by your teacher. This dictation will check your ability to spell words with *ou* and *ow*.[1]

[1] Dictate phrases and sentences from the lists on pages 51 and 52 in *How to Teach Spelling*.

/ô/—Spelled *au* and *aw*

Read and learn.

1. Use *au* at the beginning or in the middle of a word unless the /ô/ sound is followed by a single *n* or *l*; then use *aw*.
   Examples: pause because dawn lawn crawl shawl
2. Use *aw* at the end of a word for the /ô/ sound.
   Examples: saw jaw draw straw
3. Exceptions: awe awful hawk awkward Paul squawk awning lawyer hawthorn haul

Fill in the blanks with either *au* or *aw*. Then read the words. Place a check in front of the words that are exceptions to the generalizations.

h_____l	_____thor	h_____k	_____kward	g_____dy
_____ful	br_____l	s_____sage	_____tumn	s_____nter
f_____cet	bec_____se	s_____ce	appl_____d	_____ning
l_____ndry	l_____yer	p_____se	squ_____k	l_____n

Use a separate sheet of paper to write the phrases and sentences dictated by your teacher. This dictation will check your ability to spell words with *au* and *aw*.[1]

/ôt/—Spelled *aught* and *ought*

/ôt/ is spelled *aught* and *ought*.

Read and learn this nonsense sentence that contains the six *aught* words.

The farmer *caught* his *haughty, naughty daughter* and *taught* her not to *slaughter* animals.

Read and learn the seven *ought* words.

ought bought brought fought thought sought wrought

Use a separate sheet of paper to write the phrases dictated by your teacher. This dictation will check your ability to spell words with *aught* and *ought*.[2]

[1] Dictate phrases and sentences from the lists on pages 54 and 55 in *How to Teach Spelling*.
[2] Dictate phrases from the list on page 56 in *How to Teach Spelling*.

Plurals

Plurals are formed by adding *s* or *es* to the base words. When the end sound of the base word comes through your teeth, add *es*. If the end sound does not come through your teeth, add only *s*. If the base word ends in silent e, add only *s*.

wall—walls box—boxes face—faces

Read. Copy each rule and its words on a separate sheet of paper. Learn one rule at a time.

1. Words ending in *y*
   a. Words ending in *y* preceded by a vowel become plural by adding *s*.
      boy—boys play—plays
   b. Words ending in *y* preceded by a consonant become plural by changing the *y* to *i* and adding *es*.
      copy—copies cry—cries

2. Words ending in *f* or *fe*
   a. Words ending in *f* or *fe* usually become plural by adding *s*.
      chief—chiefs roof—roofs safe—safes
   b. Some words ending in *f* or *fe* become plural by changing the *f* or *fe* to *v* and adding *es*.
      calf—calves self—selves elf—elves
      scarf—scarves half—halves shelf—shelves
      knife—knives thief—thieves leaf—leaves
      wharf—wharves life—lives wife—wives
      loaf—loaves wolf—wolves

3. Words ending in *o*
   a. Words ending in *o* preceded by a vowel become plural by adding *s*.
      embryo—embryos rodeo—rodeos radio—radios
      shampoo—shampoos ratio—ratios studio—studios
   b. Most words ending in *o* preceded by a consonant become plural by adding *es*.
      buffalo—buffaloes potato—potatoes tomato—tomatoes
      Common Exceptions:
      dynamo—dynamos ditto—dittos photo—photos
      pro—pros silo—silos
   c. Words of Spanish origin, Italian musical terms, and proper names ending in *o* become plural by adding *s*.
      burro—burros bronco—broncos lasso—lassos
      poncho—ponchos pueblo—pueblos sombrero—sombreros
      soprano—sopranos piano—pianos contralto—contraltos
      cello—cellos solo—solos libretto—librettos
      Romeo—Romeos Eskimo—Eskimos Filipino—Filipinos

Plurals (continued)

4. Letters and numbers

   Letters, numbers, and signs become plural by adding *'s*.

   x's   *b*'s   7's   10's   1980's   1490's   –'s   +'s

5. Irregular plurals

   Some words form their plurals irregularly.

   child—children   man—men   woman—women
   ox—oxen   mouse—mice   louse—lice
   goose—geese   foot—feet   tooth—teeth

6. Singular and plural spellings that are the same

   Some words are the same in both the singular and the plural.

   sheep   deer   moose   species   Chinese   Japanese
   trout   salmon   grapefruit   scissors   trousers

Write the plural of the following words.

Singular	Plural	Singular	Plural
spy	______	potato	______
victory	______	loaf	______
fox	______	buffalo	______
army	______	alto	______
photo	______	display	______
wife	______	salmon	______
wharf	______	umbrella	______
supply	______	studio	______
goose	______	piano	______
worry	______	cherry	______
shelf	______	country	______
tomato	______	1900	______
couple	______	woman	______
march	______	holiday	______

Contractions

Read and learn.

A contraction is one word made from two words. One or more letters are left out when combining the two words, and those letters that are left out are replaced with an apostrophe (').

he is = he's

she is = she's

I am = I'm

I would = I'd

I will = I'll

it is = it's

is not = isn't

do not = don't

did not = didn't

does not = doesn't

cannot = can't

will not = won't

are not = aren't

was not = wasn't

were not = weren't

has not = hasn't

have not = haven't

had not = hadn't

I have = I've

he will = he'll

she will = she'll

you will = you'll

we will = we'll

here is = here's

that is = that's

what is = what's

let us = let's

who is = who's

you are = you're

you have = you've

there is = there's

they are = they're

they have = they've

they will = they'll

we are = we're

we have = we've

could not = couldn't

would not = wouldn't

should not = shouldn't

Contractions (continued)

Write the contractions for these words.

she is	________	cannot	________
had not	________	I am	________
they will	________	you will	________
let us	________	they have	________
that is	________	is not	________
are not	________	did not	________
has not	________	should not	________
it is	________	there is	________
could not	________	I will	________
they are	________	what is	________
I would	________	she will	________
does not	________	you are	________
he is	________	have not	________
we will	________	he will	________
we have	________	will not	________
do not	________	who is	________
here is	________	you have	________
were not	________	was not	________
would not	________	we are	________
I have	________		

Use a separate sheet of paper to write the sentences dictated by your teacher. This dictation will check your ability to spell contractions.[1]

[1] Dictate sentences from the list on pages 59, 60, and 61 in *How to Teach Spelling*.

The Doubling Rule (The 1-1-1 Rule)

Read and learn.

If a *one*-syllable base word ends in *one* consonant with *one* vowel before it, you must double the final consonant of the base word when adding a suffix that begins with a vowel. Do not double the final consonant if the suffix begins with a consonant.

mad	+	est	=	maddest	thin	+	ed	=	thinned
mad	+	er	=	madder	thin	+	ing	=	thinning
mad	+	ly	=	madly	thin	+	ly	=	thinly
mad	+	ness	=	madness	thin	+	ness	=	thinness

Never double the final letters *w*, *x*, and *y*.

snow + ed = snowed   box + ing = boxing   play + er = player

Join the base word and suffix to make a new word.

dim + ly = ________	fit + ed = ________
dim + ing = ________	fit + ness = ________
jog + ing = ________	hug + ed = ________
flop + y = ________	ship + ment = ________
scrub + ed = ________	quiz + ed = ________
crow + ing = ________	ship + ing = ________
bit + en = ________	big + er = ________
shred + ed = ________	fret + ful = ________
sail + ing = ________	fan + ing = ________
red + ness = ________	fret + ing = ________
fit + ful = ________	grit + y = ________
wit + y = ________	bit + er = ________

Use a separate sheet of paper to write the phrases and sentences dictated by your teacher. This dictation will check your ability to use the Doubling Rule.[1]

[1] Dictate phrases and sentences from the lists on pages 64 and 65 in *How to Teach Spelling*.

The Silent-*e* Rule

Read and learn.

When a word ends in silent e*:*

1. Drop the e before adding a suffix that begins with a vowel.
   like + able = likable
2. Keep the e before adding a suffix that begins with a consonant.
   like + ness = likeness

Exceptions to the Silent-e Rule

Read and learn.

1. Some words DROP the silent e before a suffix that begins with a consonant.

Read this nonsense sentence, copy it on a separate sheet of paper, and memorize it. It contains the nine common words that are exceptions.

Truly the ninth argument is wholly awful,[1] but the judgment and acknowledgment are duly accepted as truth.

2. Some words KEEP the silent e before a suffix that begins with a vowel. When you add the suffixes *-able* and *-ous* to words with a c or g before a final silent e, keep the silent e to keep the c and g soft.

Read, copy, and memorize.

noticeable	____________	serviceable	____________
traceable	____________	peaceable	____________
pronounceable	____________	enforceable	____________
courageous	____________	outrageous	____________
advantageous	____________	changeable	____________
chargeable	____________	manageable	____________
marriageable	____________		

[1] Adapted from Mildred B. Plunkett, *A Spelling Workbook Emphasizing Rules and Generalizations for Corrective Drill* (Cambridge, MA: Educators Publishing Service, Inc.), page 46.

3. Some words keep the silent e to preserve their identity.

dyeing (dyed)	____________	canoeing	____________
mileage	____________	hoeing	____________
acreage	____________	shoeing	____________
tingeing	____________	toeing	____________
singeing	____________		

4. The following three words that end in silent e change their spelling when you add the suffix *-ing*. They do not follow any rule. Simply memorize them.

					Past Tense						Past Tense
die	+	ing	=	dying	died	tie	+	ing	=	tying	tied
lie	+	ing	=	lying	lied						

Write eight original sentences using as many words as you can that are exceptions to the Silent-*e* Rule.

____

____

____

____

____

____

____

____

____

____

____

____

____

____

The Silent-*e* Rule (continued)

Join the base word and suffix to make a new word. Circle the exceptions to the Silent-*e* Rule.

Remember: When you add the suffixes *-able* and *-ous* to words ending with a soft c or g sound, you do not drop the silent e at the end of the word. Example: *notice* + *able* = *noticeable*.

Base Word		Suffix		New Word
acre	+	age	=	____________
praise	+	ed	=	____________
fame	+	ous	=	____________
value	+	able	=	____________
advantage	+	ous	=	____________
like	+	ness	=	____________
enforce	+	able	=	____________
continue	+	ous	=	____________
service	+	able	=	____________
canoe	+	ing	=	____________
courage	+	ous	=	____________
notice	+	able	=	____________
excite	+	ment	=	____________
manage	+	able	=	____________
charge	+	ing	=	____________
outrage	+	ous	=	____________
marriage	+	able	=	____________

Use a separate sheet of paper to write the phrases and sentences dictated by your teacher. This dictation will check your ability to use the Silent-e Rule.[1]

[1] Dictate phrases and sentences from the lists on pages 70, 71, and 72 in *How to Teach Spelling*.

/ē/—Spelled *y* and *ey*

Read and learn. Copy and learn the words.

y is a common ending for many words in English. It usually says /ē/ at the end of two- and three-syllable words.

party	__________	puppy	__________	happy	__________
candy	__________	skinny	__________	dirty	__________

ey is a far less common way of spelling the /ē/ sound at the end of words. There are only about forty of these words. The most important are:

key	__________	hockey	__________	chimney	__________
alley	__________	jockey	__________	medley	__________
attorney	__________	jersey	__________	motley	__________
donkey	__________	valley	__________	kidney	__________
monkey	__________	volley	__________	journey	__________
money	__________	galley	__________	parsley	__________
honey	__________	turkey	__________	whiskey	__________

The few common words that end in ey with ey saying /ā/ are:

they	__________	survey	__________	obey	__________
hey	__________	convey	__________	prey	__________

Use a separate sheet of paper. Write ten original sentences using as many words that end in *ey* as you can.

Use a separate sheet of paper to write the phrases dictated by your teacher. This dictation will check your ability to spell words that end in *y* and *ey*.[1]

[1] Dictate phrases from the list on page 81 in *How to Teach Spelling*.

The *Y* Rule

Read, copy, and learn.

1. If the letter before a final *y* is a vowel, the *y* doesn't change when you add a suffix.
   pl<u>a</u>y   pl<u>a</u>yed   pl<u>a</u>ying   pl<u>a</u>yful
2. If the letter before a final *y* is a consonant, the *y* changes to *i* when you add a suffix, *except* when the suffix begins with an *i*.
   car<u>ry</u>   carr<u>i</u>ed   carr<u>i</u>er   carr<u>y</u>ing

1. ____

____

____

2. ____

____

____

____

Exceptions to the *Y* Rule

Copy and learn.

day + ly = daily	______________	say + ed = said	______________
gay + ly = gaily	______________	pay + ed = paid	______________
slay becomes slain	______________	lay + ed = laid	______________
shy + ly = shyly	______________	shy + ness = shyness	______________
dry + ly = dryly	______________	dry + ness = dryness	______________
sly + ly = slyly	______________	sly + ness = slyness	______________
spry + ly = spryly	______________	spry + ness = spryness	______________

Add the suffix to the base word to make a new word.

Base Word		Suffix		New Word
delay	+	ing	=	________________
beauty	+	ful	=	________________
mislay	+	ed	=	________________
kindly	+	ness	=	________________
rely	+	ing	=	________________
study	+	ous	=	________________
modify	+	ed	=	________________
supply	+	er	=	________________

Write the base word and the suffix for the following words.

	Base Word	Suffix
carrier	________________	____________
reliable	________________	____________
annoyed	________________	____________
appliance	________________	____________
glorious	________________	____________
denies	________________	____________
prettiest	________________	____________
loneliness	________________	____________

Use a separate sheet of paper to write the phrases and sentences dictated by your teacher. This dictation will check your ability to use the *Y* Rule.[1]

Use a separate sheet of paper to write the paragraphs dictated by your teacher. This dictation is a review of all the material you have learned so far.[2]

[1] Dictate phrases and sentences from the lists on pages 83, 84, and 85 in *How to Teach Spelling*.

[2] Dictate paragraphs found on page 87 in *How to Teach Spelling*.

tion and *sion*

Read and learn.

1. The sound /shŭn/ is spelled two ways: *tion* and *sion*. If you aren't sure which to use, try *tion*; *tion* is the more commonly used form.
2. If the original word ends in *ss*, the /shŭn/ sound is always spelled *sion* (memorize the spelling of these words).

confess = confession	process = procession
depress = depression	profess = profession
discuss = discussion	progress = progression
express = expression	recess = recession
impress = impression	regress = regression
possess = possession	success = succession

3. /shŭn/ is spelled *cion* in two words:

   coercion suspicion
4. /chŭn/ is spelled *tion* in these few words:

   question mention attention contention
5. /chŭn/ is spelled *sion* in words such as:

   extension suspension expansion comprehension apprehension
6. If you hear /zhŭn/ in a word, it can only be spelled *sion*.

   television explosion confusion
7. /shŭn/is spelled *xion* in the word *complexion*.

Which end sounds do you hear in these words? Fill in the blanks with /shŭn/, /chŭn/, or /zhŭn/.

mention ____________	subtraction ____________	question ____________
emotion ____________	possession ____________	succession ____________
attention ____________	division ____________	direction ____________
ambition ____________	education ____________	television ____________
exclusion ____________	objection ____________	explosion ____________
procession ____________	impression ____________	prevention ____________
election ____________	conclusion ____________	comprehension ____________

Fill in the blanks with *tion*, *sion*, or *cion*, and write the number of the reason you chose each ending.

The reason for choosing a particular ending should be one of the following:

1. The original word ends in *ss* . . . so we use *sion*.
2. The ending says /shŭn/ . . . so we use *tion*.
3. The ending says /chŭn/ . . . so we use *tion* or *sion*.
4. The ending says /zhŭn/ . . . so we use *sion*.
5. Exceptions: *coercion, suspicion* . . . so we use *cion*.

Remember: /shŭn/ is spelled *tion* as in *station*.
/chŭn/ is spelled *tion* as in *question*.
/shŭn/ is spelled *sion* if the word to which it is added ends in *ss*.
/chŭn/ is spelled *sion* as in *comprehension*.
/zhŭn/ is spelled *sion* as in *television*.
/shŭn/ is spelled *xion* as in *complexion*.

Add Ending	Reason	Add Ending	Reason
addi tion	2	explo____	____
confu____	____	conten____	____
coer____	____	succes____	____
protec____	____	comprehen____	____
subtrac____	____	diver____	____
discus____	____	suspi____	____
exten____	____	atten____	____
ques____	____	conclu____	____
solu____	____	transfu____	____
inva____	____	apprehen____	____
expres____	____	objec____	____
pollu____	____	provi____	____

Use a separate sheet of paper to write the phrases and sentences dictated by your teacher. This dictation will check your ability to spell words that end with *tion* and *sion*.[1]

[1] Dictate phrases and sentences from the lists on pages 89 and 90 in *How to Teach Spelling*.

The *i*-before-*e* Generalization

Read, copy, and learn. **Copy**

Put i before e ______________________

Except after c ______________________

Or when sounded like /ā/ ______________________

As in neighbor and weigh. ______________________

Use a separate sheet of paper to copy all the words in this lesson. Read, copy, and learn the first group of words. Look up the meaning of any word you do not know.

Put *i* before e

1. chief
   thief
   brief
   achieve
   retrieve
   reprieve

   handkerchief

   mischief
   grief
   belief
   relief

   mischievous
   grieve
   believe
   relieve

Do not move on to word groups 2, 3, and 4 until you can write group 1 from memory.

2. niece
   piece
   pierce
   fierce

3. field
   shield
   wield
   yield

4. pier
   tier
   cashier
   frontier

After you have learned to spell and to write from memory all the words in groups 1, 2, 3, and 4, read, copy, and learn the words in groups 5 and 6. Notice that in group 6, *ie* does not say /ē/.

5. fiend
   priest
   shriek
   siege
   besiege
   hygiene

6. friend
   sieve
   view
   review
   interview

Except after *c*

1. ceiling
   receipt
   receive

2. conceit
   deceit
   conceive
   deceive
   perceive

After you have learned to spell and to write from memory all the *i*-before-*e* words and all the except-after-*c* words, read, copy, and learn the words spelled *ei* that are sounded like /ā/.

Or when sounded like /ā/

1. eight
   weight
   freight

2. weigh
   sleigh
   neigh
   neighbor

3. vein
   veil
   skein
   rein
   reindeer
   reign

   their
   beige
   heir
   heiress
   feign
   deign
   inveigle

Exceptions to the *i*-before-*e* Generalization

Read, copy, and learn this nonsense sentence, which contains six of the exceptions spelled *ei*.

Neither leisured foreigner seized the weird height.[1]
(either) (leisure) (foreign) (seize)

More exceptions spelled with *ei* to copy and learn. Look up the meaning of any word you do not know.

forfeit
counterfeit
caffeine
protein
sheik
surfeit
sovereign
heifer
sleight

More exceptions to copy and learn. In these exceptions, *ie* comes after *c*.

ci says /sh/ in these words

ancient
glacier
species
conscience

fici says /fish/ in these words

efficient
deficient
sufficient
proficient

[1] **Mildred B. Plunkett, *A Spelling Workbook for Corrective Drill for Elementary Grades* (Cambridge, MA: Educators Publishing Service, Inc.), page 66.**

The *i*-before-*e* Generalization (continued)

Fill in the blanks with either *ie* or *ei*. Then read the words.

Exercise 1		*Exercise 2*	
v____n	ach____ve	h____ght	shr____k
v____l	p____r	y____ld	br____f
b____ge	front____r	fr____nd	____ght
rel____f	cash____r	h____fer	c____ling
n____ce	ch____f	l____sure	profic____nt
bel____ve	misch____f	rec____pt	rev____w
w____ght	v____w	prot____n	____ther
sh____ld	fr____ght	gr____ve	caff____ne
f____ld	n____ghbor	effic____nt	surf____t
retr____ve	f____rce	sl____ght	n____ther
th____f	th____r	t____r	n____gh

Exercise 3

sl____gh	f____nd	consc____nce	s____ve
p____ce	perc____ve	dec____t	for____gner
forf____t	pr____st	defic____nt	spec____s
conc____t	w____rd	suffic____nt	rec____ve
glac____r	s____ze	dec____ve	anc____nt
conc____ve	counterf____t	bes____ge	r____gn

Use a separate sheet of paper to write the phrases and sentences dictated by your teacher. This dictation will check your ability to spell words with *ie* and *ei*.[1]

[1] Dictate phrases and sentences from the lists on pages 94 and 95 in *How to Teach Spelling*.

Possessive Words

Read and learn.

Possessive words show ownership or relationship.

1. Singular possessive
   a. Singular words become possessive by adding 's.
      baby's crib   child's tray   boss's office   princess's crown   Gus's dog
2. Plural possessive
   a. Plural words ending in s add only an apostrophe.
      babies' toys   princesses' crowns
   b. Other plural words become possessive by adding 's.
      children's room   mice's tracks
3. Possessive personal pronouns
   a. Possessive personal pronouns do not need an apostrophe.
      its   his   hers   ours   yours   theirs

Write each of the following words in the correct column.

class's	merchant's	man's	heiress's
sleigh's	glasses'	nieces'	priests'
wives'	thieves'	princess's	cashier's
neighbor's	jockey's	foreigners'	student's
friend's	men's	babies'	Davises'
children's	sailors'	Davis's	heifers'

Singular Possessive Words		Plural Possessive Words	
class's			

Silent Letters

Many words contain letters that are not pronounced. They may have been pronounced at one time, but our language has changed through usage. Through your reading you are probably familiar with many of these words.

Read and learn. Copy the words on a separate sheet of paper. Look up in a dictionary any word you cannot define.

b is not sounded in these words:
doubt, debt, comb, dumb, thumb, tomb, lamb, climb, crumb, numb, plumber, bomb.

c is not sounded in these words:
scene, scent, science, scissors, scythe.

g is not sounded in these words:
gnat, gnash, gnarl, gnaw, gnome, sign, assign, design, resign, align, benign, malign, diaphragm.

h is not sounded in these words:
hour, honor, exhaust, exhibit, vehicle, rhyme, rhythm, rhinoceros, rhubarb, rhapsody, rhetoric, rheumatic, rheumatism, ghost, ghetto, ghoul, ghastly, gherkin, herb.

k is not sounded in these words:
knee, know, knowledge, known, knew, knife, knit, knot, knob, knock, knight, kneel, knuckle, knack, knead, knave, knoll, knapsack.

l is not sounded in these words:
folk, yolk, balk, talk, walk, chalk, stalk, calf, calves, half, halves.

n is not sounded in these words:
condemn, hymn, column, autumn, solemn.

p is not sounded in these words:
receipt, raspberry, corps, cupboard, pneumonia, pseudonym, psychiatry, psychology.

s is not sounded in these words:
isle, island, aisle.

t is not sounded in these words:
often, listen, hasten, fasten, moisten, glisten, christen.

u is not sounded in these words:
build, built, buy, guess, guest, guide, guard, guilt, guild, guitar, guarantee, guerrilla, plague, rogue, vogue, tongue, league.

w is not sounded in these words:
answer, whole, sword, write, written, wrote, wrap, wreath, wreck, wrong, wrist, wrench, wrinkle, wring, wrung, wren, wretched, wrought, wrath, wrangle, wrangler, writhe.

In the following exercises, write next to each word the letter or letters that are silent in the word.

Exercise 1		*Exercise 2*		*Exercise 3*	
wreath	______	debt	______	write	______
knit	______	talk	______	knee	______
comb	______	hymn	______	numb	______
sign	______	sword	______	knot	______
listen	______	wrap	______	gnaw	______
column	______	solemn	______	know	______
hasten	______	scent	______	knife	______
ghost	______	wrong	______	gnat	______
thumb	______	exhibit	______	scene	______
doubt	______	ghastly	______	rhubarb	______
island	______	answer	______	yolk	______
wrote	______	walk	______	hour	______
honor	______	rhapsody	______	often	______
guard	______	wrist	______	knew	______
plumber	______	climb	______	fasten	______
lamb	______	crumb	______	limb	______
dumb	______	guess	______	condemn	______
wrong	______	buy	______	scissors	______
whole	______	kneel	______	bomb	______
moisten	______	guilt	______	knob	______
build	______	chalk	______	known	______

Use a separate sheet of paper to write the sentences dictated by your teacher. This dictation will check your ability to spell words with silent letters.[1]

[1] Dictate sentences from the list on pages 100, 101, and 102 in *How to Teach Spelling*.

The Doubling Rule, Part II

Review the Doubling Rule for one-syllable words on page 23. On a separate sheet of paper, write the Doubling Rule from memory.

Read, copy, and learn the Doubling Rule, Part II, for words with two or more syllables.

Double the final consonant of the base word when adding a suffix that begins with a vowel if the following conditions apply:
1. the last syllable is accented (stressed),
2. the last syllable ends in one consonant with only one vowel before it, and
3. the suffix you are adding begins with a vowel.

1.

2.

3.

It is helpful to know that prefixes are not usually accented. Also, if the last syllable is mit, it is almost always accented.

Examples:

ad/mit´	+	ance	=	admittance
oc/cur´	+	ence	=	occurrence
com/pel´	+	ed	=	compelled
com/mit´	+	ing	=	committing
per/mit´	+	ed	=	permitted
gal´/lop	+	ed	=	galloped

Read and learn.

Words containing the stem *fer*

1. These words *never double* the final consonant. The accent is on the first syllable; therefore, the Doubling Rule does not apply.
   offer suffer differ
2. Other words containing the stem *fer* double the final consonant only when you add the suffixes *-ed, -al,* and *-ing.*
   prefer + ed = preferred prefer + able = preferable
3. The stem *fer* adds the suffixes *-ent, -ence,* and *-ency,* never *-ant, -ance,* and *-ancy.*

Words containing the stem *fit*

1. These words *never double* the final consonant. The accent is on the first syllable; therefore, the Doubling Rule does not apply.
   profit benefit discomfit
2. These words double the final consonant when you add a suffix beginning with a vowel.
   befit + ing = befitting
   unfit + ed = unfitted
   outfit + ing = outfitting
   refit + ing = refitting
   misfit + ed = misfitted

Test yourself. On a separate sheet of paper, see if you can write from memory the rules for the stems *fer* and *fit.*

Exercise 1

Directions: 1. Divide the word into syllables.
2. Place an accent mark after the accented syllable.
3. Write the complete word, adding the suffix.

Word		Suffix		New Word
dif'|fer	+	ence	=	difference
unfit	+	ing	=	______________
refer	+	able	=	______________
refit	+	ed	=	______________
outfit	+	ed	=	______________

The Doubling Rule, Part II (continued)

Exercise 2

Directions: 1. Divide the word into syllables.
2. Place an accent mark after the accented syllable.
3. Write the complete word, adding the suffix.

Word		Suffix		New Word
forget	+	ing	=	______________________
confer	+	ed	=	______________________
limit	+	ing	=	______________________
profit	+	ing	=	______________________
propel	+	er	=	______________________
regret	+	able	=	______________________
submit	+	ed	=	______________________
forbid	+	en	=	______________________
excel	+	ed	=	______________________
equip	+	ing	=	______________________
patrol	+	ed	=	______________________
forgot	+	en	=	______________________
suffer	+	ing	=	______________________
transfer	+	ing	=	______________________
acquit	+	al	=	______________________
forget	+	able	=	______________________
excel	+	ent	=	______________________
occur	+	ence	=	______________________
visit	+	ing	=	______________________
commit	+	ed	=	______________________

Exercise 3

Directions: 1. Divide between the base word and the suffix.
2. Write the base word.
3. Write the suffix.

	Base Word	Suffix
transfer|ence	transfer	ence
thundering	__________	________
profited	__________	________
differing	__________	________
benefited	__________	________
shivering	__________	________
difference	__________	________
offered	__________	________
blundered	__________	________
concurred	__________	________
reference	__________	________
suffered	__________	________
numbering	__________	________
slanderer	__________	________
differed	__________	________
opened	__________	________
equipment	__________	________
visited	__________	________
deserted	__________	________

Use a separate sheet of paper to write the phrases and sentences dictated by your teacher. This dictation will check your ability to use the Doubling Rule, Part II.[1]

[1] Dictate phrases and sentences from the lists on pages 106 and 107 in *How to Teach Spelling*.

*Review Exercise 1—Doubling Rule, Parts I and II, Silent-*e *Rule,* Y *Rule*

Directions: **1. Write the base word and suffix for each word below. Indicate the rule that applies to each word. Mark exceptions to rules with a check.**
2. Use these abbreviations:

d = Doubling Rule | **se = Silent-*e* Rule**
d II = Doubling Rule, Part II | **y = *Y* Rule**

	Base Word	Suffix	Rule	Exception
scarred	scar	ed	d	
daily	day	ly	y	✓
scared				
gladly				
occupying				
nervous				
merrily				
preferred				
profited				
shyness				
achievement				
satisfied				
forgiven				
likeness				
obeyed				
equipped				
forgotten				
changeable				
wholly				
business				

*Review Exercise 2—Doubling Rule, Parts I and II, Silent-*e *Rule,* Y *Rule*

Directions: 1. Divide all two-syllable words and place an accent after the correct syllable.
2. Write the new word, adding the suffix.
3. Indicate which rule applies to the word:
d = Doubling Rule se = Silent-*e* Rule
d II = Doubling Rule, Part II y = *Y* Rule
4. Mark exceptions to rules with a check.

	New Word	Rule	Exception
con|trol´ + ing	controlling	dII	
cou´|rage + ous	courageous	se	✓
bury + ing			
extreme + ly			
use + able			
thin + ly			
pay + ed			
scar + ed			
blunder + ed			
refer + al			
slop + y			
marry + age			
outrage + ous			
transfer + able			
mad + ness			
benefit + ed			
excite + ed			
quiet + ed			
manage + able			
offer + ing			

/ŭs/—Spelled *us* and *ous*

Read, copy, and learn.

us is usually a noun ending.

____

ous is an adjective suffix. It is sometimes added to a noun to make an adjective.

____

____

These three words are contractions. Memorize them.

wondrous	monstrous	disastrous
______________	______________	______________
(wonder)	(monster)	(disaster)

Learn the following words.

Nouns

focus	exodus
minus	octopus
cactus	syllabus
radius	abacus
genius	terminus
bonus	alumnus
census	stimulus
fungus	isthmus
sinus	hippopotamus
crocus	narcissus
lotus	omnibus
circus	hibiscus

Adjectives

dangerous	miscellaneous
strenuous	miraculous
humorous	ridiculous
continuous	thunderous
enormous	contagious
joyous	mysterious
nervous	courageous
copious	fabulous
porous	outrageous
famous	perilous
numerous	mountainous
hazardous	rigorous
marvelous	victorious

Celsius

Exercise

Directions: Place the following words in the correct column.

cactus, nervous, terminus, genius, miscellaneous, radius, alumnus, enormous, ridiculous, crocus, omnibus, porous, thunderous, bonus, contagious, victorious, abacus, octopus, mysterious, outrageous, disastrous, fungus, Celsius, fabulous, minus, humorous, continuous, census, sinus, narcissus, monstrous, hazardous, courageous

us	*ous*
__________	__________
__________	__________
__________	__________
__________	__________
__________	__________
__________	__________
__________	__________
__________	__________
__________	__________
__________	__________
__________	__________
__________	__________
__________	__________
__________	__________
__________	__________
__________	__________
	__________

Use a separate sheet of paper to write the phrases and sentences dictated by your teacher. This dictation will check your ability to spell words with *us* and *ous*.[1]

[1] Dictate phrases and sentences from the lists on pages 109 and 110 in *How to Teach Spelling*.

Latin Stems *cede, ceed, sede, cess*

Read and learn.

The following words come from the Latin stems *cede* and *cess.*

1. *ceed* is used in three words. Copy them.

exceed ______________ proceed ______________ succeed ______________

2. *cede* is used in most words. Copy the following words.

accede ______________ recede ______________

concede ______________ secede ______________

intercede ______________ procedure ______________
(Note how this spelling differs from that of the word *proceed.*)

precede ______________

3. Only one word is spelled with *sede*. Copy it.

supersede ______________

4. These words use the stem *cess*. Copy them.

abscess ______________ process ______________

recess ______________ access ______________

excess ______________ success ______________

Exercise

Write five original sentences using *exceed, proceed, succeed, supercede,* and *procedure.*

____

____

____

____

____

Use a separate sheet of paper to write the sentences dictated by your teacher. This dictation will check your ability to spell words that end in *cede, ceed, sede,* and *cess.*[1]

[1] Dictate sentences from the list on pages 111 and 112 in *How to Teach Spelling.*

/kŭl/—Spelled *cal* and *cle*

Read, copy, and learn.

cal is an adjective ending.

---

cle is a noun ending.

Read the words, copy them on a separate sheet of paper, and learn them.

Adjectives—*cal*

chemical[1]	practical	electrical	theatrical	medical
nautical	clinical	satirical	lyrical	vertical
chronological	political	ethical	theological	musical[1]
optical	comical	symmetrical	magical	vocal
classical	radical[1]	fiscal	tropical	mystical
physical[1]	cubical	tactical	mechanical	whimsical
clerical	reciprocal	logical	typical	alphabetical

Nouns—*cle*

article	follicle	bicycle	oracle	uncle
circle	obstacle	cuticle	spectacle	vehicle
cubicle	particle	miracle		

Use a separate sheet of paper to write the phrases and sentences dictated by your teacher. This dictation will check your ability to spell words that end in *cal* and *cle*.[2]

[1] This word is also a noun.

[2] Dictate phrases and sentences from the lists on pages 114 and 115 in *How to Teach Spelling*.

/ŭl/—Spelled *al* and *el*

Read this chapter. Copy the first section on a separate sheet of paper and learn it. Then move on to the next section. Copy and learn it.

Because *-al* and *-el* sound similar, it helps to know that:

1. *-al* is usually an adjective ending.
   -al can also be a noun ending when it is added to a verb to form a noun (*approve—approval*).

Adjectives

brutal	literal	occasional	secretarial
several	fatal	regal	factual
total[1]	exceptional	royal	structural
national	local	rural	testimonial[1]
normal	mental	maternal	remedial
general[1]	neutral	paternal	animal[1]
verbal	natural[1]	fraternal	criminal[1]
universal	central	feudal	rival[1]
oval[1]	frugal	recessional[1]	mortal[1]
moral[1]	penal	capital[1]	signal[1]
vital	cordial[1]	accidental	pedal[1]
liberal[1]	personal	industrial	material[1]
original[1]	legal		

Verbs to Nouns

approval	denial	refusal	rehearsal
acquittal	proposal	trial	appraisal
renewal	rebuttal	reversal	arrival
betrayal	recital	disposal	

[1] **This word is also a noun.**

2. *-el* is usually an ending for words that act as nouns or as both nouns and verbs. Some of these words also act as adjectives.

Nouns

chapel	novel[1]	kernel	colonel
hovel	vessel	caramel	satchel
bowel	flannel[1]	lapel	mongrel[1]
hotel	sequel	weasel	scoundrel
morsel	bushel	sentinel	personnel
camel	damsel	squirrel	mackerel

Nouns and Verbs

kennel	funnel	swivel	parallel[1]
libel	marvel	label	pommel
panel	parcel	model[1]	shovel
jewel	rebel[1]	quarrel	travel
barrel	trowel	channel	tunnel
chisel	level[1]	enamel	

Use a separate sheet of paper. Write ten original sentences using as many words as you can that end in *al* and *el.*

Use a separate sheet of paper to write the phrases and sentences dictated by your teacher. This dictation will check your ability to spell words that end in *al* and *el.*[2]

[1] This word is also an adjective.

[2] Dictate phrases and sentences from the lists on pages 117 and 118 in *How to Teach Spelling*.

The Suffixes *-able* and *-ible*

Pronouncing words that end in /ŭbl/ does not help you decide whether to spell the ending *able* or *ible*. The rules given below will help you decide. Always follow the rules in the order given.

Copy the words. Work from left to right.

1. Use *-able* if a corresponding *-ation* word exists.

-ation Words		→	*-able* Words	
consideration	________		considerable	________
adoration	________		adorable	________
vegetation	________		vegetable	________
imagination	________		imaginable	________
application	________		applicable	________
duration	________		durable	________
navigation	________		navigable	________
valuation	________		valuable	________
separation	________		(in)separable	________
toleration	________		(in)tolerable	________
variation	________		variable	________
dispensation	________		(in)dispensable	________
taxation	________		taxable	________
admiration	________		admirable	________
adaptation	________		adaptable	________
operation	________		operable	________
communication	________		communicable	________

2. Use *-ible* if you cannot think of an *-ation* word but can think of a *-tion* or *-sion* word.

-tion or *-sion* Words		→	*-ible* Words	
admission	______________		admissible	______________
apprehension	______________		apprehensible	______________
comprehension	______________		comprehensible	______________
conversion	______________		convertible	______________
division	______________		divisible	______________
extension	______________		extensible	______________
reversion	______________		reversible	______________
accession	______________		accessible	______________
audition	______________		audible	______________
collection	______________		collectible	______________
corruption	______________		corruptible	______________
digestion	______________		digestible	______________
ignition	______________		ignitible	______________
instruction	______________		instructible	______________
connection	______________		connectible	______________
destruction	______________		destructible	______________

3. If you cannot make the first two guidelines work, then follow this rule:
Use *-able* to turn a verb or noun into an adjective.

Verbs/Nouns		→	Adjectives	
break	______________		breakable	______________
move	______________		movable	______________
cure	______________		curable	______________
suit	______________		suitable	______________
fashion	______________		fashionable	______________
comfort	______________		comfortable	______________

The Suffixes *-able* and *-ible* (continued)

4. Use *-ible* to keep c or g soft.

Soft c		Soft g	
forcible	____________	tangible	____________
enforcible	____________	negligible	____________
producible	____________	legible	____________
reducible	____________	illegible	____________
coercible	____________	eligible	____________
invincible	____________	dirigible	____________
convincible	____________	incorrigible	____________

5. Copy and learn these exceptions.

possible	____________	gullible	____________
sensible	____________	credible	____________
resistible	____________	incredible	____________
irresistible	____________	horrible	____________
collapsible	____________		

Exercise 1

Use a separate sheet of paper. Write from memory the four rules you should follow to help you decide whether to use *-able* or *-ible* as a suffix for words that end with the sound /ŭbl/. Then write the nine exceptions from memory.

____________________ ____________________

____________________ ____________________

____________________ ____________________

____________________ ____________________

____

Exercise 2

Directions: A. Fill in the blanks with *able* or *ible*.
B. Write the number of the reason for your choice.
1. *-ation* word
2. *-tion* or *-sion* word
3. verb or noun to adjective
4. to keep *c* or *g* soft

-able or *-ible*	1, 2, 3, or 4
invinc ible	4
unforgett____	____
neglig____	____
insepar____	____
prevent____	____
compar____	____
admir____	____
break____	____
permiss____	____
intellig____	____
justifi____	____
perish____	____
elig____	____
surmount____	____
divis____	____
convert____	____
digest____	____

Use a separate sheet of paper to write the phrases and sentences dictated by your teacher. This dictation will check your ability to spell words that end in *able* and *ible*.[1]

[1] Dictate phrases and sentences from the lists on pages 120 and 121 in *How to Teach Spelling*.

The Suffixes *-ance, -ant, -ancy* and *-ence, -ent, -ency*

It is often difficult to know how to spell the following suffixes: *-ance* or *-ence, -ant* or *-ent,* and *-ancy* or *-ency*. The following five rules will help you make the correct choice.

On the facing page, copy and learn the following rules and words. Copy and learn all of sections 1 and 2 before moving on to copy and learn sections 3, 4, and 5.

Use the suffixes *-ance, -ant,* and *-ancy*:

1. <u>when you can think of a related word ending in *-ation.*</u>

toleration	tolerance	tolerant	
radiation	radiance	radiant	radiancy
variation	variance	variant	
precipitation	precipitance	precipitant	precipitancy
domination	dominance	dominant	
hesitation	hesitance	hesitant	hesitancy
participation		participant	

(There are many more of these words.)

2. <u>to change verbs to nouns.</u>

rely	reliance	reliant
perform	performance	
insure	insurance	
assure	assurance	
resemble	resemblance	
annoy	annoyance	
ignore	ignorance	ignorant
acquaint	acquaintance	

(There are many more of these words.)

Use the suffixes *-ance, -ant,* and *-ancy*:

1. ______________________________

(There are many more of these words.)

2. ______________________________

(There are many more of these words.)

The Suffixes *-ance, -ant, -ancy* (continued)

Use the suffixes *-ance, -ant,* and *-ancy*:

3. to keep the c and g hard in these words.

extravagance	extravagant
arrogance	arrogant
significance	significant
elegance	elegant

4. for these words, which are usually nouns that name people.

defendant	
lieutenant	
accountant	
attendant	
descendant	
occupant	occupancy
applicant	
sergeant	
tenant	tenancy
assailant	
truant	truancy
inhabitant	

Exceptions: president, resident, superintendent

5. for these three contractions.

hinder	hindrance
enter	entrance
remember	remembrance

Use the suffixes *-ance, -ant,* and *-ancy:*

3. ______________________________

______ ______

______ ______

______ ______

______ ______

4. ______________________________

______

______

______

______

______

______ ______

______

______

______ ______

______

______ ______

______

Exceptions: ______, ______, ______

5. ______________________________

______ ______

______ ______

______ ______

The Suffixes *-ence, -ent, -ency* (continued)

Now you are ready to read, copy, and learn when to use the suffixes *-ence, -ent,* and *-ency*. There are ten rules that apply to these suffixes. On the facing page, copy and learn rules 1 through 10. Be sure you know the rule and the spelling of each word in each section before you move on to the next rule.

Use the suffixes *-ence, -ent,* and *-ency:*

1. after a stem ending in *i.*

audi	audience		
bedi	obedience	obedient	obediency
peri	experience		
veni	convenience	convenient	
pedi	expedience	expedient	expediency
fici		deficient	deficiency
		sufficient	sufficiency
		proficient	proficiency
		efficient	efficiency
leni		lenient	leniency
pati	patience	patient	
	impatience	impatient	

2. after *qu.*

	consequence	consequent	
	eloquence	eloquent	
	frequence	frequent	frequency
	sequence	sequent	
		delinquent	delinquency

Use the suffixes *-ence, -ent,* and *-ency:*

1. ______________________________

2. ______________________________

The Suffixes *-ence, -ent, -ency* (continued)

Use the suffixes *-ence, -ent,* and *-ency:*

3. to keep c and g soft.

convergence	convergent	
contingence	contingent	contingency
diligence	diligent	
indulgence	indulgent	
	indecent	indecency
innocence	innocent	
magnificence	magnificent	
reminiscence	reminiscent	
reticence	reticent	reticency
	urgent	urgency
	stringent	stringency
	translucent	translucency

4. with the *escent* group.

incandescence	incandescent
adolescence	adolescent
convalescence	convalescent
phosphorescence	phosphorescent
effervescence	effervescent
iridescence	iridescent
fluorescence	fluorescent

Use the suffixes *-ence, -ent,* and *-ency:*

3. ______________________________

4. ______________________________

The Suffixes *-ence, -ent, ency* (continued)

Use the suffixes *-ence, -ent,* and *-ency:*

5. after the Latin stem *fer,* "to bear."
(The Latin stem *fer* has already been learned in The Doubling Rule, Part II.)

	conference		
	reference	referent	
	deference		
	transference		
	inference		
	preference		
	difference	different	
Exception:	sufferance		

6. after the Latin stem *sist,* "to stand."

	subsistence	subsistent	
	persistence	persistent	
	insistence	insistent	
	consistence	consistent	consistency
	existence	existent	
Exceptions:	assistance	assistant	
	resistance	resistant	
	desistance		

7. after the Latin stem *min,* "to jut."

	prominence	prominent
	eminence	eminent
	imminence	imminent

Use the suffixes *-ence, -ent,* and *-ency:*

5. ______________________________
(The Latin stem *fer* has already been learned in The Doubling Rule, Part II.)

Exception:

6. ______________________________

Exceptions:

7. ______________________________

The Suffixes *-ence, -ent, -ency* (continued)

Use the suffixes *-ence, -ent,* and *-ency:*

8. after the Latin stem *haer,* "to stick."

adherence	adherent
coherence	coherent
incoherence	incoherent
inherence	inherent

9. after the Latin stem *cur,* "to run."

	current
occurrence	
concurrence	concurrent
recurrence	recurrent

10. after the Latin stem *spond,* "to promise."

respondence	respondent	respondency
correspondence	correspondent	
despondence	despondent	despondency

Use a separate sheet of paper to write the phrases and sentences dictated by your teacher. This dictation will check your ability to spell words that end in *ance, ant, ancy* and *ence, ent, ency.*[1]

[1] **Dictate phrases and sentences from the lists on pages 126 and 127 in *How to Teach Spelling.***

Use the suffixes *-ence, -ent,* and *-ency:*

8. ______________________________

9. ______________________________

10. ______________________________

/ĕns/—Spelled *ense*

ense is part of the stem of a word. It sounds the same as *-ence,* but it is not a suffix. Almost every *ense* word is on the list below.

Read, copy, and learn the following *ense* words and their derivatives.

ense Words		Derivatives	
incense	__________		
license	__________		
dense	__________	density	__________
condense	__________	condensation	__________
defense	__________	defensive	__________
offense	__________	offensive	__________
immense	__________	immensity	__________
dispense	__________	dispensation	__________
expense	__________	expensive	__________
recompense	__________		
suspense	__________	suspension	__________
sense	__________	sensitive	__________
		insensitive	__________
nonsense	__________	nonsensical	__________
tense	__________	tension	__________
intense	__________	intensive	__________
pretense	__________	pretension	__________
		pretentious	__________

Use a separate sheet of paper to write the phrases and sentences dictated by your teacher. This dictation will check your ability to spell words with *ense.*[1]

[1] Dictate phrases and sentences from the lists on pages 128 and 129 in *How to Teach Spelling.*

The /sh/ Sound

Words with the /sh/ sound are often difficult to spell. The following list will help familiarize you with the various spellings for this sound.

Read and learn.

What says /sh/?

1. *s* says /sh/ in the words *sure* and *sugar*. Learn them.
2. *sh* says /sh/ as in *ship*.
3. *ch* says /sh/ in words of French derivation such as *chef* and *charade*.
4. *ce* says /sh/ in the word *ocean* and a few scientific words.
5. *si* says /sh/ when it begins an ending (*-sion, -sial, -sient*).
   The only common word ending in *-sial* is *controversial*.
   The only common word ending in *-sient* is *transient*. Learn to spell these two words.
6. *ti* says /sh/ when it begins an ending (*-tion, -tial, -tient, -tious, -tian*.)
7. *ci* says /sh/ when it begins an ending (*-cion, -cial, -cient, -cious, -cian*).

In this lesson you will learn how to decide whether to use *ti* or *ci* to say /sh/ at the beginning of a word ending. There is no dependable rule to help you choose the correct spelling for the /sh/ sound. However, you can usually figure out whether to use *ti* or *ci* at the beginning of an ending if either *t* or c is in the stem of the original word.

Read the following examples.

face—fa*c*ial	confiden*t*—confiden*t*ial
grace—gra*c*ious	infec*t*—infec*t*ious
finance—finan*c*ial	poten*t*—poten*t*ial
music—musi*c*ian	substitu*t*e—substitu*t*ion

Copy and memorize these four exceptions.

benefit—beneficial

________________—________________

technique—technician

________________—________________

palace—palatial

________________—________________

substance—substantial

________________—________________

The /sh/ Sound (continued)

Exercise

See if you can add the correct ending, beginning with either *ti* or *ci,* to the following words.

Original Word	Word with Ending	Original Word	Word with Ending
space	__________	sacrifice	__________
president	__________	potent	__________
part	__________	face	__________
commerce	__________	vice	__________
infect	__________	torrent	__________
office	__________	different	__________
race	__________	society	__________
artifice	__________	suspicion	__________

Read, copy, and memorize the following rules and words.

1. When a noun ends in *ence*, its adjective must end in *ential*.

____

____

Nouns		Adjectives	
essence	__________	essential	__________
confidence	__________	confidential	__________
consequence	__________	(in)consequential	__________
prudence	__________	prudential	__________
residence	__________	residential	__________
influence	__________	influential	__________
preference	__________	preferential	__________

The following two nouns that end in *ance* have adjectives that end in *antial*. Memorize them.

Nouns		Adjectives	
circumstance	__________	circumstantial	__________
substance	__________	substantial	__________

2. The ending *-ician* usually denotes a person skilled in some particular art or science. The original words often end in *ic* or *ics*.

____

____

____

magician	__________	physician	__________
optician	__________	technician	__________
musician	__________	politician	__________
beautician	__________	obstetrician	__________
mathematician	__________	statistician	__________
electrician	__________	pediatrician	__________

3. The following words have no companion words. Memorize them.

ancient	__________	nuptial	__________
Martian	__________	celestial	__________
special	__________	credential	__________
glacial	__________	patient	__________
luscious	__________	impatient	__________
pretentious	__________	quotient	__________
initial	__________	delicious	__________

Use a separate sheet of paper to write the phrases and sentences dictated by your teacher. This dictation will check your ability to spell words with the /sh/ sound.[1]

[1] Dictate phrases and sentences from the lists on pages 132 and 133 in *How to Teach Spelling*.

The /er/ Sound

The most common way to spell the /er/ sound is *er*. However, the /er/ sound can also be spelled *ar, ir, our, ur,* and *ear*. It is difficult to choose the correct spelling. The best way is to learn each spelling of the /er/ sound separately.

1. a. *-ar* says /er/.

Check the nouns and adjectives in which *ar* says /er/ that you use most often. Memorize them, be able to recite them, and write them from memory for your teacher.

Nouns			Adjectives		
calendar	hangar	poplar	lunar	granular	muscular
dollar	registrar	nectar	solar	circular	polar
beggar	bursar	cedar	secular	globular	stellar
mortar	pillar	vicar	angular	singular	similar
grammar	seminar	collar	vulgar	jugular	peculiar
pedlar	vinegar	cellar	popular	familiar	regular
burglar	caterpillar				
liar	nectarine				

b. *-ard* says /erd/.

Memorize the underlined words. Be able to write and recite them from memory.

lizard	wizard	tankard	orchard	scabbard	custard
drunkard	haggard	standard	blizzard	buzzard	mustard

c. *-ward* says /werd/.

Memorize the underlined words. Be able to write and recite them from memory.

inward	southward	seaward	upward	forward	coward
outward	eastward	awkward	downward	backward	steward
onward	westward	windward	northward	homeward	

2. -er says /er/.

a. -*er* is the most common suffix that says /er/.

Memorize the three reasons below that tell how -*er* is used. Be able to write them from memory. Read each of the following words, and check those that you do not know how to spell or define. Write each of your checked words on a separate sheet of paper and learn to spell them. Show the paper to your teacher.

1) -*er* denotes one's occupation or family relationship.

baker	welder	barber	swimmer	father	geographer
lawyer	runner	reporter	driver	golfer	sister
gardener	mother	officer	laborer	producer	brother
teacher	farmer	player			

2) -*er* is added to nouns and adjectives of place.

islander	foreigner	Londoner	villager	southerner	New Yorker

3) -*er* shows comparative degree.

milkier	smaller	larger	kinder	thinner	stouter
colder	shorter	bigger	shorter	slimmer	greater
hotter	taller	wilder	fatter		

b. *er* is the usual way to spell the /er/ sound in the middle syllable of a word.

property	mineral	internal	governor	general	liberal
refrigerate	energy	reversal	internal	every	several
kindergarten		literal			

3. -*ir* says /er/.

Check the words in which *ir* says /er/ that you use most often. Memorize them and be able to recite them from memory.

confirm	skirmish	stir	squirm	third	flirt
shirt	thirsty	circle	whirl	bird	thirty
virtue	squirt	girl	girdle	skirt	dirt
birch	birthday	swirl	chirp	thirteen	twirl
squirrel	sirloin	dirge	sir	fir	first
firm					

The /er/ Sound (continued)

4. <u>*or* says /er/.</u>

Memorize the four reasons below that tell when *or* is used for the /er/ sound. Be able to write them from memory. Read each of the following words, and check those that you do not know how to spell or define. Write each of your checked words on a separate sheet of paper and learn to spell them. Show the paper to your teacher.

a. After a *w* the /er/ sound is spelled *or*.

worship	word	worse	work	work	worry
worthy	world	worm	worth		

b. Add the suffix *-or* to a companion verb to make a noun. (You can hear the /t/ sound before the /er/ sound.)

illustrate	illustrator	indicate	indicator
moderate	moderator	operate	operator
refrigerate	refrigerator	equate	equator
decorate	decorator	investigate	investigator
navigate	navigator	radiate	radiator
incubate	incubator	imitate	imitator
legislate	legislator	translate	translator
percolate	percolator	instigate	instigator
duplicate	duplicator	vibrate	vibrator

c. Add the suffix *-or,* which says /er/, to words ending in *s* or *t* that are derived from Latin stems. (You can hear the /t/ sound before the /er/ sound.)

contract	contractor	deposit	depositor
tract	tractor	assess	assessor
act	actor	profess	professor
conduct	conductor	debt	debtor
inspect	inspector	audit	auditor
protect	protector	instruct	instructor
invent	inventor	confess	confessor
construct	constructor	fact	factor
collect	collector	credit	creditor

d. Many abstract nouns end in *or*.

pallor	splendor	error	minor	valor	labor
humor	glamor	major	color	favor	terror

5. *our* says /er/ in words of French derivation.

Memorize the following words. Be able to write them from memory.

courteous	nourishment	sojourn	courageous	flourish	nourish
adjourn	journey	courage	journal	scourge	

6. *ur* says /er/.

Read each of the following words, and check the words that you do not know how to spell or define. Write each of your checked words on a separate sheet of paper and learn to spell them. Show the paper to your teacher.

furnish	hurl	surprise	hurt	surgeon	curl
sulphur	purser	furl	purpose	survive	refurbish
excursion	blur	spur	nocturnal	hurdle	disturb
Saturday	Thursday	burn	turtle	suburb	purse
nurse	gurgle	perturb	further	curt	curfew
purple	surmount	auburn	spurn	turn	surf
absurd	occur	church	fur	murder	surpass
urge	lurk	sturdy			

7. *ear* says /er/.

Memorize the following words. Be able to write them from memory.

early	search	yearn	learn	rehearse	earn
pearl	research	heard	hearse	rehearsal	earth
earnest					

Use a separate sheet of paper to write the sentences dictated by your teacher. This dictation will check your ability to spell words with the /er/ sound.[1]

[1] Dictate sentences from the list on pages 137 and 138 in *How to Teach Spelling*.

The Suffixes *-ary*, *-ery*, and *-ory*

The suffixes *-ary*, *-ery*, and *-ory* cause confusion because the spelling usually cannot be determined by pronunciation. You must memorize the words that use each suffix.

Look up the definition of any word you do not know. Write the word and definition on a separate sheet of paper. Show it to your teacher. Learn to spell all the words. It is best to learn one group at a time before moving on to the next group of words.

Read, copy, and learn.

<u>*-ary*</u>

1. The suffix *-ary* is used for both adjectives and nouns.
   a. As an adjective suffix, *-ary* usually means "pertaining to" or "connected with."

____

____

____

Adjectives

hereditary	________________	literary	________________
customary	________________	culinary	________________
pulmonary	________________	necessary	________________
secondary	________________	solitary	________________
visionary	________________	contrary	________________
arbitrary	________________	elementary	________________
extraordinary	________________	imaginary	________________
temporary	________________	sanitary	________________
momentary	________________	monetary	________________
dietary	________________	voluntary	________________
veterinary	________________	supplementary	________________
honorary	________________	stationary	________________

b. When *-ary* is a noun suffix, it denotes a person, place, or thing.

____

____

Nouns

infirmary	____________	secretary	____________
ovary	____________	estuary	____________
beneficiary	____________	penitentiary	____________
vocabulary	____________	apothecary	____________
centenary	____________	diary	____________
salary	____________	sanctuary	____________
itinerary	____________	dictionary	____________
commentary	____________	glossary	____________
library	____________	notary	____________
aviary	____________	dignitary	____________

2. The following words that end in *-ary* may be used both as adjectives and nouns.

____

____

capillary	____________	obituary	____________
reactionary	____________	incendiary	____________
auxiliary	____________	tributary	____________
subsidiary	____________	missionary	____________
adversary	____________	rotary	____________
primary	____________	contemporary	____________
military	____________	ordinary	____________
revolutionary	____________	judiciary	____________
anniversary	____________	summary	____________

-ery

1. The noun suffix *-ery* is largely identified with business or occupational terms. It denotes not only the business or occupation itself but also the place of business, or the article produced or sold.

____

____

____

____

archery	______	stationery	______
grocery	______	bakery	______
refinery	______	nursery	______
embroidery	______	machinery	______
celery	______	hosiery	______
artillery	______	pottery	______
winery	______	cannery	______
hatchery	______	distillery	______
delivery	______	cemetery	______
finery	______	scenery	______

2. The suffix *-ery* is used in the following abstract words.

____

____

flattery	______	imagery	______
mockery	______	drudgery	______
thievery	______	misery	______
bravery	______	trickery	______
robbery	______	forgery	______
mastery	______	slavery	______
		mystery	______

-ory

1. The great majority of words ending in *-ory* are adjectives. The suffix is usually preceded by *s* or *t*.

____

____

____

-tory Adjectives

mandatory	____________	obligatory	____________
preparatory	____________	satisfactory	____________
contradictory	____________	explanatory	____________
transitory	____________	migratory	____________
derogatory	____________	introductory	____________
exclamatory	____________	expository	____________

-sory Adjectives

promissory	____________	sensory	____________
compulsory	____________	cursory	____________

2. The following are a few nouns that end in *ory*. The suffix is usually preceded by *s* or *t*.

laboratory	____________	dormitory	____________
factory	____________	territory	____________
victory	____________	inventory	____________
directory	____________	memory	____________
history	____________	accessory	____________
lavatory	____________	trajectory	____________
observatory	____________	theory	____________

Use a separate sheet of paper to write the phrases and sentences dictated by your teacher. This dictation will check your ability to spell words that end in *ary, ery,* and *ory*.[1]

[1] Dictate phrases and sentences from the lists on pages 140 and 141 in *How to Teach Spelling*.

Homonyms

Read, copy, and learn.

Homonyms are words that sound the same but have different meanings and spellings.

1. Read the following list of homonyms. Put a check next to any of the words you cannot define. Then look them up in the dictionary and write them with their definitions on a separate sheet of paper. Show them to your teacher.
2. On a separate sheet of paper write original sentences using the starred words and their homonym or homonyms. You may use more than one of these words in any sentence.

List of Homonyms

ail—ale	air—heir	*aisle—isle
all—awl	*allowed—aloud	alter—altar
arc—ark	*assent—ascent	ate—eight
bail—bale	bait—bate	ball—bawl
base—bass	be—bee	*beach—beech
bear—bare	beat—beet	beer—bier
bell—belle	*birth—berth	blew—blue
*board—bored	*bolder—boulder	bow—bough
bread—bred	break—brake	bridle—bridal
browse—brows	*bury—berry	by—bye—buy
*capital—capitol	carrot—carat—caret	cast—caste
ceiling—sealing	cellar—seller	*cereal—serial
cheap—cheep	choir—quire	clause—claws
cord—chord	core—corps	*course—coarse
creak—creek	cue—queue	current—currant
dear—deer	desert—dessert	die—dye
done—dun	dough—doe	due—dew—do

*duel—dual
fair—fare
flee—flea
fort—forte
fur—fir
gilt—guilt
*groan—grown
hair—hare
heard—herd
him—hymn
hour—our
idol—idle
*kernel—colonel
knot—not
leak—leek
lesson—lessen
lone—loan
mail—male
marshal—martial
metal—mettle
need—knead
nose—knows
pain—pane
pause—paws
peddle—pedal
piece—peace
pole—poll
prey—pray
raise—raze
red—read
right—write—rite
roam—Rome

earn—urn
fawn—faun
*flew—flue—flu
foul—fowl
gate—gait
great—grate
guessed—guest
hall—haul
here—hear
hoard—horde
hue—hew—Hugh
in—inn
knew—new
know—no
led—lead
liar—lier—lyre
lynx—links
main—mane—Maine
maze—maize
minor—miner
night—knight
oar—or—ore
pale—pail
peak—peek
peel—peal
plain—plane
pore—pour
*principal—principle
*rapped—wrapped—rapt
reel—real
ring—wring
roll—role

faint—feint
feet—feat
flower—flour
four—for
gild—guild
Greece—grease
hail—hale
heal—heel
hi—high
hoarse—horse
I—eye
its—it's
knit—nit
lain—lane
lee—lea
lie—lye
made—maid
*mantle—mantel
meet—meat
naval—navel
none—nun
one—won
passed—past
pear—pair—pare
peer—pier
please—pleas
*presence—presents
rain—reign—rein
read—reed
rest—wrest
road—rode—rowed
route—root

Homonyms (continued)

row—roe
seem—seam
sell—cell
serf—surf
*sight—site—cite
sole—soul
sore—soar
stayed—staid
*straight—strait
*taught—taut
tear—tier
*thrown—throne
told—tolled
veil—vale
wave—waive
wear—ware
whose—who's
wrote—rote

rows—rose
seen—scene
sense—cents
sheer—shear
slay—sleigh
some—sum
stair—stare
steak—stake
sweet—suite
*tea—tee
there—their—they're
*to—too—two
turn—tern
wait—weight
way—weigh
week—weak
would—wood
yoke—yolk

sale—sail
*sees—seas—seize
sent—cent—scent
shown—shone
so—sew—sow
son—sun
*stationary—stationery
steel—steal
tale—tail
team—teem
*threw—through
toe—tow
vane—vain—vein
*waste—waist
we—wee
whole—hole
*wretch—retch

Prefixes

A prefix is a vowel or a group of letters placed at the beginning of a word to change the meaning of the word.

un in front of *lucky* = *unlucky*

Some prefixes change their spelling to adapt to the word to which they are being added. They do this to make them easier to say and more pleasant to hear.

Learn each prefix, its changes, if it has any, and its meaning. A successful way to do this is to copy the prefixes and their meanings on a separate sheet of paper and memorize them. Learn four or five every day until you have learned them all. Show your prefix paper to your teacher. Then test yourself by writing them from memory on another sheet of paper.

List of Prefixes

Prefix	Meaning	Example
1. *a-*	on, in, at	afloat, asleep
2. *ab-*	from	absent
3. *ad-*	to, toward	adjust
spelled *ac* before *c*		accede
spelled *ac* before *k*		acknowledge
spelled *ac* before *qu*		acquaint
spelled *af* before *f*		affix
spelled *ag* before *g*		aggravate
spelled *al* before *l*		allow
spelled *an* before *n*		annex
spelled *ap* before *p*		append
spelled *ar* before *r*		arrive
spelled *as* before *s*		assemble
spelled *at* before *t*		attract
4. *ambi-*	both	ambidextrous
5. *ante-*	before	antecedent
6. *anti-*	opposite, against	antidote, antiaircraft

Prefixes (continued)

Prefix	Meaning	Example
7. *be-*	by, about	because, before
8. *circum-*	around	circumference
9. *com-*	together, with	combine
spelled *con* before all consonants except *b, f, h, l, m, p,* and *r*		connect, conduct
spelled *co* before *vowels*		co-operate
spelled *co* before *h*		cohere
spelled *co* before *gn*		cognitive
spelled *col* before *l*		collide
spelled *com* before *b*		combine
spelled *com* before *f*		comfort
spelled *com* before *m*		communicate
spelled *com* before *p*		compress
spelled *cor* before *r*		corrode
10. *contra-*	against	contradict
11. *de-*	down, from, away	descent, decline
12. *dis-*	apart, away	discriminate, discard
spelled *di* sometimes		divert
spelled *dif* before *f*		different
13. *en-*	in	engrave, enthrone
14. ex-	out of	exclude
spelled e sometimes		evaporate
spelled *ec* before *c*		eccentric
spelled *ef* before *f*		efficient
15. *extra-*	outside of, beyond	extraordinary, extracurricular
16. *for-*	prohibit, apart	forbid, forget
17. *fore-*	front, before	forehead

Prefix	Meaning	Example
18. *in-*	not, in	inactive, inhabit
spelled *il* before *l*		illusion
spelled *im* before *b*		imbibe
spelled *im* before *m*		immigrate
spelled *im* before *p*		imprison
spelled *ir* before *r*		irrigate
19. *inter-*	between	intercept
20. *mis-*	wrong	misfit, misuse
21. *ne-*	no, not	necessary
spelled *neg* sometimes		negative
22. *non-*	not	nonresident
23. *ob-*	to, toward	object
	in the way of, against	obscure
spelled *oc* before *c*		occur
spelled *of* before *f*		offend
spelled *op* before *p*		opponent
24. *out-*	out, beyond	outcast, outside
25. *over-*	over	overcoat, overtime
26. *per-*	through	pervade, perfect
27. *post-*	after	postdate, postgraduate
28. *pre-*	before	precede, prevent
29. *pro-*	before, forward, instead of	propose, proceed, pronoun
30. *re-*	go back	recall, rewrite
31. *se-*	apart	secede, seclude
spelled *sed* sometimes		sedition

Prefixes continued on next page.

Prefixes (continued)

	Prefix	Meaning	Example
32.	*sub-*	under	subway
	spelled *suc* before *c*		succumb
	spelled *suf* before *f*		suffer
	spelled *sug* before *g*		suggest
	spelled *sum* before *m*		summation
	spelled *sup* before *p*		suppress
	spelled *sus* before *c*		susceptible
	spelled *sus* before *p*		suspend
	spelled *sus* before *t*		sustain
33.	*super-*	above, beyond	supernatural
34.	*trans-*	across, beyond	transfer
	spelled *tra* sometimes		traverse
35.	*un-*	not	unable, unlock
36.	*under-*	under, below	underground

Word Categories

The following lists of words are organized in categories because each group of words follows a particular spelling pattern. These words are not pronounced or spelled phonetically.

The following instructions apply to all the word categories. Follow steps 1, 2, and 3 for each category.

1. **Read, copy, and learn all the words in each category. Look up in a dictionary the definition of any word you cannot define.**
2. **On a separate sheet of paper use all the starred words in each category in original sentences that show their meaning.**
3. **After each category has been studied, use a separate sheet of paper to write the phrases and sentences dictated by your teacher. These dictations will check your ability to spell the words correctly.**

/k/—Spelled *que*

In these words of French derivation, /k/ is spelled *que*.

*opaque	______	antique	______
*bisque	______	*critique	______
*clique	______	physique	______
*plaque	______	picturesque	______
*pique	______	*grotesque	______
*unique	______	technique	______
*oblique	______	*humoresque	______

Your teacher will dictate phrases and sentences from the lists on page 149 in *How to Teach Spelling*. Omit sentence 2.

/k/—Spelled *ch*

In these words of Greek derivation, /k/ is spelled *ch*.

ache	____________	mechanic	____________
echo	____________	schedule	____________
choir	____________	architect	____________
*chaos	____________	*orchid	____________
scheme	____________	character	____________
anchor	____________	technical	____________
chord	____________	orchestra	____________
school	____________	*schooner	____________
choral	____________	chemistry	____________
chorus	____________	scholastic	____________
stomach	____________	*psychiatrist	____________
*monarch	____________	*technique	____________
chronic	____________	*chronological	____________
scholar	____________		

Your teacher will dictate phrases and sentences from the lists on pages 147 and 148 in *How to Teach Spelling*.

/zher/—Spelled *sure*

Spelling these three words with the /zher/ sound can be troublesome.

Read, copy, and learn them.

measure	____________	pleasure	____________
treasure	____________		

Your teacher will dictate phrases and sentences from the lists on page 152 in *How to Teach Spelling*.

/cher/—Spelled *ture*

The following words end in /cher/; /cher/ is spelled *ture.*

mixture ______________________

nature ______________________

capture ______________________

*nurture ______________________

pasture ______________________

*culture ______________________

posture ______________________

feature ______________________

fixture ______________________

*rapture ______________________

*rupture ______________________

future ______________________

*gesture ______________________

*suture ______________________

picture ______________________

torture ______________________

*venture ______________________

*miniature ______________________

adventure ______________________

moisture ______________________

agriculture ______________________

*conjecture ______________________

*overture ______________________

creature ______________________

literature ______________________

departure ______________________

puncture ______________________

fracture ______________________

furniture ______________________

scripture ______________________

sculpture ______________________

temperature ______________________

structure ______________________

manufacture ______________________

legislature ______________________

In the following words /ch/ is spelled *tu.*

century ______________________

natural ______________________

Portugal ______________________

spatula ______________________

tarantula ______________________

mature ______________________

fluctuate ______________________

Your teacher will dictate phrases and sentences from the lists on pages 150 and 151 in *How to Teach Spelling.*

/ĭt/ and /āt/—Spelled *ate*

In the following nouns and adjectives /ĭt/ is spelled *ate*.

*deliberate	______	*desolate	______
immaculate	______	temperate	______
fortunate	______	senate	______
private	______	illiterate	______
*appropriate	______	chocolate	______
immediate	______	separate	______
elaborate	______	desperate	______
graduate	______	*palate	______
delicate	______	duplicate	______
*predicate	______	*subordinate	______
climate	______	considerate	______
pirate	______	*frigate	______

In these and other verbs /āt/ is spelled *ate*.

*appropriate	______	operate	______
graduate	______	duplicate	______
punctuate	______	separate	______
*desolate	______	*fluctuate	______
*subordinate	______	*orchestrate	______
*saturate	______	*reiterate	______
*elaborate	______	*deliberate	______

These three words end in *ite; ite* says /ĭt/. Copy and learn them.

definite ______ favorite ______ infinite ______

Your teacher will dictate phrases and sentences from the lists on pages 152, 153, and 154 in *How to Teach Spelling.*

/ĭv/—Spelled *ive*

In the following words /ĭv/ is spelled *ive*.

comparative	__________	detective	__________
expensive	__________	effective	__________
constructive	__________	*alternative	__________
sensitive	__________	successive	__________
adhesive	__________	*decisive	__________
explosive	__________	inventive	__________
*cohesive	__________	*conducive	__________
*persuasive	__________	*retentive	__________
*affirmative	__________	automotive	__________
digestive	__________	narrative	__________
communicative	__________	creative	__________
preventive	__________	positive	__________
cursive	__________	negative	__________
*instinctive	__________	attentive	__________

Your teacher will dictate phrases and sentences from the lists on pages 155 and 156 in *How to Teach Spelling.*

/ū/ or /o͞o/—Spelled *ew* or *ue*

In the following words /ū/ or /o͞o/ is spelled *ew* or *ue*.

ew

dew ______	*hew ______	nephew ______
new ______	*pew ______	*curfew ______
grew ______	stew ______	*askew ______
few ______	knew ______	

ue

argue ______	statue ______	avenue ______
due ______	value ______	*subdue ______
sue ______	tissue ______	continue ______
cue ______	*issue ______	*virtue ______
*hue ______	rescue ______	barbecue ______

Your teacher will dictate phrases and sentences from the lists on pages 157, 158, and 159 in *How to Teach Spelling.*

/yo͞o wŭl/, /cho͞o wŭl/, and /o͞o wŭl/—Spelled *ual*

In the following words /yo͞o wŭl/, /cho͞o wŭl/, and /o͞o wŭl/ are spelled *ual*.

actual ______	*habitual ______
*manual ______	individual ______
usual ______	annual ______
mutual ______	*effectual ______
punctual ______	*perpetual ______
*factual ______	*eventual ______
gradual ______	spiritual ______
	casual ______

Your teacher will dictate phrases and sentences from the lists on pages 159 and 160 in *How to Teach Spelling.*

/ŭn/, /yŭn/, /jŭn/, and /ēŭn/—Spelled *ion*

In the following words /ŭn/, /yŭn/, /jŭn/, and /ēŭn/ are spelled *ion*.

cushion	____________	*stallion	____________
fashion	____________	rebellion	____________
*battalion	____________	union	____________
companion	____________	reunion	____________
*communion	____________	region	____________
*dominion	____________	religion	____________
*medallion	____________	accordion	____________
opinion	____________	champion	____________
onion	____________	scorpion	____________
*pavilion	____________	*oblivion	____________

Your teacher will dictate phrases and sentences from the lists on pages 160 and 161 in *How to Teach Spelling*.

/ēŭn/—Spelled *ian*

In the following words /ēŭn/ is spelled *ian*.

*custodian	____________	*pedestrian	____________
guardian	____________	*ruffian	____________
historian	____________	Bostonian	____________
librarian	____________	Philadelphian	____________

Your teacher will dictate phrases and sentences from the lists on pages 161 and 162 in *How to Teach Spelling*.

/ĭs/—Spelled *ice*

In the following words /ĭs/ is spelled *ice*.

*avarice	______	*poultice	______
justice	______	practice	______
*precipice	______	*malice	______
notice	______	*novice	______
service	______	apprentice	______

Your teacher will dictate phrases and sentences from the lists on pages 156 and 157 in *How to Teach Spelling.*

/ĭz ŭm/—Spelled *ism*

In the following words /ĭz ŭm/ is spelled *ism*.

*atheism	______	*communism	______
heroism	______	*plagiarism	______
criticism	______	*mysticism	______
*egotism	______	nationalism	______
patriotism	______	*feudalism	______
mechanism	______		

Your teacher will dictate phrases and sentences from the lists on page 162 in *How to Teach Spelling.*

-ept, -act, -ect, -ict

The following words may cause confusion—some because of their spelling, and some because of their definitions.

Copy each group of words and learn to spell each word. Write a definition for each word on a separate sheet of paper.

-ept	Copy Word
crept	____________
kept	____________
swept	____________
accept	____________
slept	____________
except	____________
wept	____________

-act	Copy Word
act	____________
tract	____________
react	____________
attract	____________
exact	____________
contract	____________
refract	____________

-ect	Copy Word
direct	____________
retrospect	____________
affect	____________
select	____________
connect	____________
elect	____________
prospect	____________

-ect	Copy Word
defect	____________
effect	____________
respect	____________
detect	____________
suspect	____________
expect	____________

-ict	Copy Word
predict	____________
derelict	____________
evict	____________

-ict	Copy Word
verdict	____________
district	____________
restrict	____________

Your teacher will test you on the spelling of these words.

Notes